Sacred Songs of Christmas

In the beginning was the Word,

and the Word was with God,

and the Word was God …

and the Word became flesh and dwelt among us,

and we have seen His glory,

glory as of the only Son from the Father,

full of grace and truth.

JOHN 1:1, 14 ESV

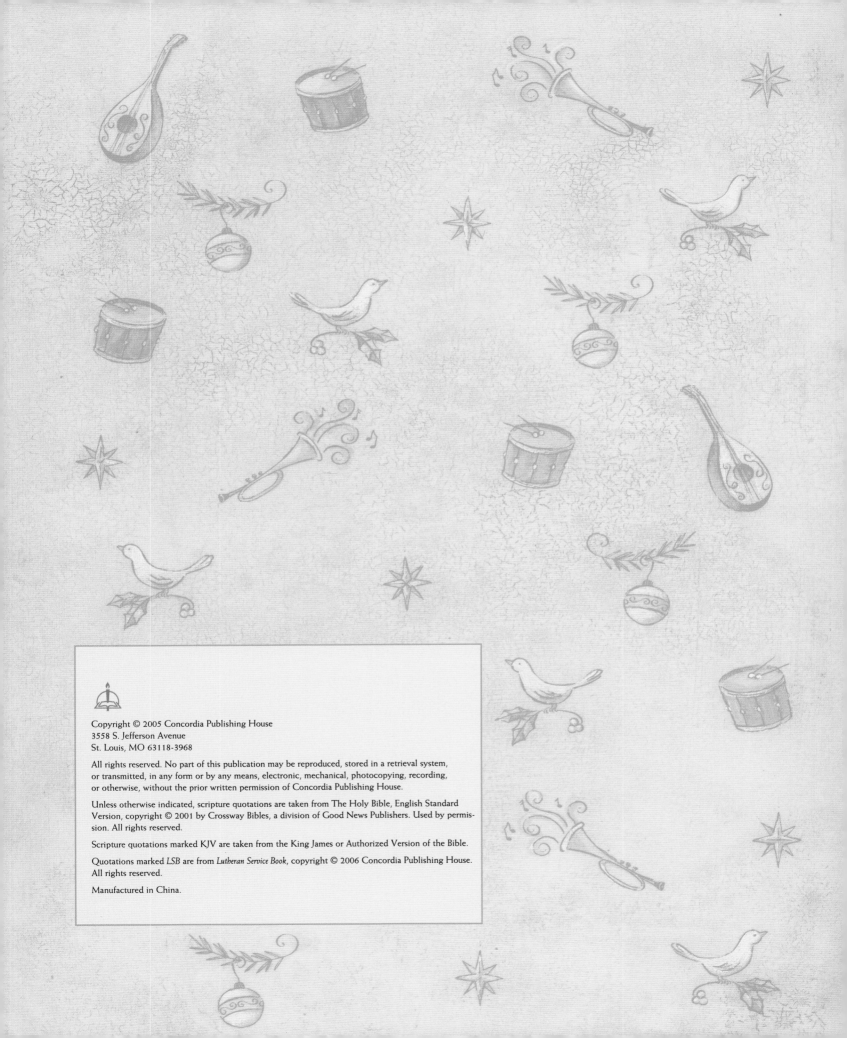

Sacred Songs of Christmas

A FAMILY TREASURY

ILLUSTRATIONS BY

ANDREA EBERBACH ✳ PAINE PROFFITT ✳ NICOLE WONG

CONCORDIA PUBLISHING HOUSE • SAINT LOUIS

Introduction

Our Lord God has given us the remarkable gift of music to use as we worship, praise, and celebrate Jesus' birth at Christmas. The songs of Christmas take many forms. They are soft and contemplative. They are joyous and exuberant. They are uncomplicated and pure.

This collection of songs, stories, poems, Scripture passages, and artwork has been gathered to help your family prepare for and celebrate the Christ Child's birth. Read the stories, listen to the music, and rejoice in the greatest gift to all the world —the gift of our Savior, Jesus Christ.

Table of Contents

The Angel Gabriel

God had made a promise. God promised that He would send a Savior for His people. Faithful people knew their heavenly Father would keep His promises to His children—so they waited.

Day after day, year in and year out, they worked and played, they lived and worshiped. And they waited … thousands of years … for the promised Savior to arrive. And He did!

But imagine the surprise of the young Jewish girl when the angel of the Lord told her that, at last, the Messiah was coming and she was chosen to be His mother. From all the women in all the world throughout all time—the Savior was to be born to her.

As this classic Christmas hymn reminds us, the humble girl believed and she placed her trust and her future in God's hands.

1 The an - gel Ga - bri - el from heav - en came,
2 "For know a bless - ed moth - er thou shalt be,
3 Then gen - tle Mar - y meek - ly bowed her head;
4 Of her, Em - man - u - el, the Christ, was born

With wings as drift - ed snow, with eyes as flame:
All gen - er - a - tions laud and hon - or thee;
"To me be as it pleas - eth God," she said.
In Beth - le - hem all on a Christ - mas morn,

"All hail to thee, O low - ly maid - en Mar - y,
Thy Son shall be Em - man - u - el, by seers fore - told,
"My soul shall laud and mag - ni - fy God's ho - ly name."
And Chris - tian folk through - out the world will ev - er say:

Most high - ly fa - vored la - dy."
Most high - ly fa - vored la - dy." Glo - ri - a!
Most high - ly fa - vored la - dy,
"Most high - ly fa - vored la - dy,"

Text: Basque carol, para. Sabine Baring–Gould, 1834–1924
Tune: GABRIEL'S MESSAGE, Basque carol

The Magnificat

And Mary said,
"My soul magnifies the Lord,
    and my spirit rejoices in God my Savior,
for He has looked on the humble estate of His servant.
    For behold, from now on all generations
        will call me blessed;
for He who is mighty has done great things for me,
    and holy is His name.
And His mercy is for those who fear Him
    from generation to generation.
He has shown strength with His arm;
    He has scattered the proud in the thoughts
        of their hearts;
He has brought down the mighty from their thrones
    and exalted those of humble estate;
He has filled the hungry with good things,
    and the rich He has sent empty away.
He has helped His servant Israel,
    in remembrance of His mercy,
as He spoke to our fathers,
    to Abraham and to his offspring forever."

Luke 1:46–55

As man longs for a light on a dark night, so God's believing people of long ago waited and looked for the coming of the Light of the World, Jesus, the Desire of all nations. One by one, through the prophets of old, lights began to appear in man's world of darkness.

From *Jesus, Joy of Man's Desiring*

And it came to pass in those days, that there went out a decree from Caesar Augustus, that all the world should be taxed. (*And* this taxing was first made when Cyrenius was governor of Syria.) And all went to be taxed, every one into his own city.

And Joseph also went up from Galilee, out of the city of Nazareth, into Judaea, unto the city of David, which is called Bethlehem; (because he was of the house and lineage of David:) To be taxed with Mary his espoused wife, being great with child.

And so it was, that, while they were there, the days were accomplished that she should be delivered. And she brought forth her firstborn son, and wrapped Him in swaddling clothes, and laid Him in a manger; because there was no room for them in the inn.

Luke 2:1–7 KJV

At Christmas time He came to earth,

The infant Son of Mary mild,
And angel voices sang with mirth,
The Son of God, the Holy Child.

From *He Came*

Saint Nicholas

How many Santa Clauses have you seen this week? Did you know that Santa Claus is based on a man who really lived in the fourth century in Asia Minor (present-day Turkey)? The man was Nicholas, a Christian pastor.

The story is told of a poor family that had three daughters who wanted to be married. A dowry, or a treasure of money and valuable items to set up a home, was needed before a daughter could be married. To help the family, Nicholas dropped three bags of gold coins through the window one night. Soon people heard about Nicholas's kind deed and started to imitate him by dressing in the vestments of a bishop as they gave gifts to others.

Nicholas died on December 6, and Christians remember him and the way God worked through him to bring the good news of Jesus and His love. In Europe, people remember Nicholas as Father Christmas; in North America, we call him Santa Claus.

No matter how we know or remember Nicholas, his love and kind deeds can remind us of the great love God has for us in sending His Son, Jesus, to die on the cross for our salvation.

From *Emmanuel, God with Us!*

Angels We Have Heard on High

And there were in the same country shepherds abiding in the field, keeping watch over their flock by night. And, lo, the angel of the Lord came upon them, and the glory of the Lord shone round about them: and they were sore afraid. And the angel said unto them, Fear not: for, behold, I bring you good tidings of great joy, which shall be to all people. For unto you is born this day in the city of David a Saviour, which is Christ the Lord. And this *shall be* a sign unto you; Ye shall find the babe wrapped in swaddling clothes, lying in a manger. And suddenly there was with the angel a multitude of the heavenly host praising God, and saying,

Glory to God in the highest,
and on earth peace,
good will toward men.

ANGELS WE HAVE HEARD ON HIGH

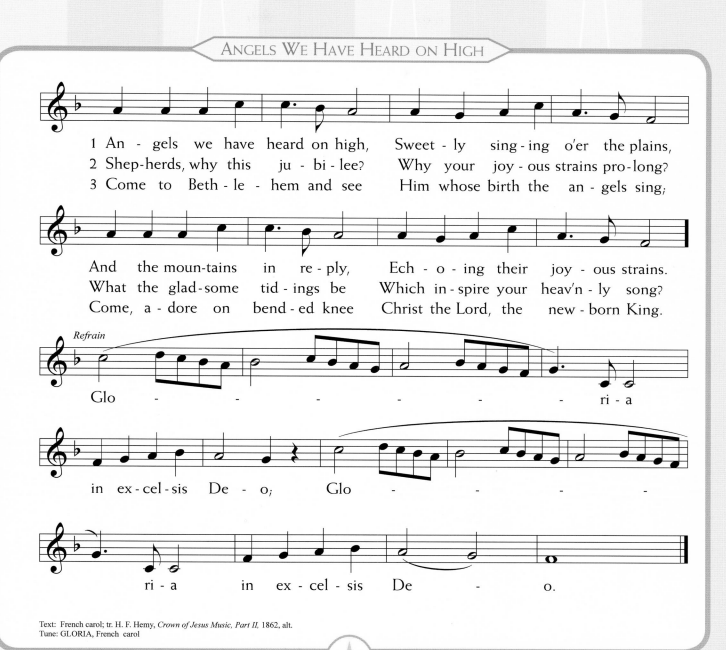

1 An - gels we have heard on high, Sweet - ly sing - ing o'er the plains,
2 Shep-herds, why this ju - bi - lee? Why your joy - ous strains pro-long?
3 Come to Beth - le - hem and see Him whose birth the an - gels sing;

And the moun-tains in re - ply, Ech - o - ing their joy - ous strains.
What the glad-some tid - ings be Which in - spire your heav'n - ly song?
Come, a - dore on bend - ed knee Christ the Lord, the new - born King.

Refrain

Glo - - - - - - ri - a

in ex - cel - sis De - o; Glo - - - - -

ri - a in ex - cel - sis De - o.

Text: French carol; tr. H. F. Hemy, *Crown of Jesus Music, Part II,* 1862, alt.
Tune: GLORIA, French carol

Long ago one holy night

Angels filled the sky with light.
They came to bring good news of love
To men on earth from God above.

"Christ is born, the Lord of all.
Find Him in a cattle stall."
"He brings true peace to men on earth:
Oh, praise God for the Savior's birth."

Shepherds heard this wondrous story,
Heard the angels singing, "Glory"—
"Glory to the Lord above:
God has shown to all His love."

"In Bethlehem," the angel said,
"You shall find the Christ Child's bed."
The shepherds hurried to find Him then;
They hurried fast to Bethlehem.

They found Him lying on the hay
Just as they'd heard the angel say.
Mary, His mother, watched Him there;
The Baby Jesus, sweet and fair.

The shepherds were so very glad
For the visit that they had.
They told the people everywhere
About the Christ Child lying there.

They told the people how they went
To see the Savior God had sent.
They thanked the Lord, and so do we,
That Jesus the Savior came to be.

God wanted all the men on earth
To know the story of Christ's birth.
He sent a star with special light,
A star to shine for Christ each night.

Far in the East some Wise Men stood
And said, "This star means God is good."
"A new King God has sent to earth;
Let's go and find His place of birth."

They traveled then a long, long way
To find the place where Jesus lay.
They were so glad their gifts to bring
To Christ, their Savior and their King!

Gold, frankincense, and myrrh they gave
To Him who came their souls to save.
They worshiped Him as Lord of all
The heaven and earth, this Baby small.

FROM *GIFTS FOR JESUS*

The angel Gabriel appears to a young girl to tell her she will be the mother of God's Son. Nine months later the angel choir of heaven announces to shepherds the birth of the Messiah.

The greatest good news to come to all mankind, that God in His mercy was sending Jesus to be the Savior of the world, comes on the wings of God's angels. This is not the work of cherubic figures with harp and bow, but the majestic work given to God's mighty messengers.

A messenger is "one who is sent" to speak on behalf of another or to perform a deed or action on behalf of another. From humanity's point of view, angels are indeed God's agents, sent from God's side to do His will and service among us. Besides describing the function of the angels, the Greek word for messenger becomes the English name for them.

These messengers are the angels of God, charged with the care of men (Psalm 91). Created at the dawn of time, the angels have witnessed every action of God on mankind's behalf and every era of our existence. As the true and loyal messengers of God, angels always act as an extension of His will and affection toward humanity.

Angels have no physical form; they are not flesh and blood. The Bible indicates that angels are most often invisible to human eyes. However, God allows His messengers to appear visibly to aid in their contacts with the human race. When visible, the angel is described as having the appearance of a man. (Read Genesis 18:1–2 and Genesis 19:1–5 as examples of Scripture's description of angels.) The visible appearance of angels is so strongly associated with normal human form and appearance that the writer of Hebrews states some people "have entertained angels unawares" (Hebrews 13:2).

Scripture also portrays angelic visitations as stunning occurrences. In most instances when appearing visibly, angels are so glorious and impressively beautiful that they amaze and terrify those who witness their presence. Matthew describes the angel who rolled the stone away from Christ's tomb as dressed in a white garment that shone like a flash of brilliant lightning. Notice the effect the angel had on those who witnessed him: "And for fear of him the guards trembled and became like dead men" (Matthew 28:4).

The angels were created by God to attend to the work and the person of His Son, Jesus Christ. On the first Christmas, the infant Jesus was born into the world of man for our redemption. While glorious and remarkable, it is not surprising that an entire heavenly choir of angels appears on that night to sing, "Glory to the newborn king; Peace on earth and mercy mild, God and sinners reconciled!"

Scot Kinnaman

Angel Ornament Craft

Materials

- ★ 20 inches of 4-inch wide gathered lace
- ★ 10 inches of 1-inch wide gathered lace
- ★ 7/8-inch wood bead
- ★ Craft hair
- ★ 1 square of white felt
- ★ Paint or markers for eyes and lips
- ★ Craft wire
- ★ Braided cord
- ★ Twine or fishing line for hanging
- ★ Hot glue gun

Directions

1. Tightly gather the 4-inch lace on craft wire and twist the ends of the wire to form the dress.

2. Hot glue the bead to the top of the gathered lace.

3. Gather the 1-inch lace on craft wire to form the collar. Wrap the wire around the base of the head and twist the ends of the wire closed.

4. Cut felt into the shape of a butterfly to make wings. Use hot glue gun to glue braided cord around the edges of the wings.

5. Glue craft hair to the top of the head.

6. Cut a piece of braided cord for a halo and glue the ends to form a circle. Glue the halo to the top of the head.

7. Knot a piece of twine or fishing line to make a hanger. Glue the hanger on top of the wings with the loop above the wings.

8. Paint or draw eyes and mouth on the head to make the face.

9. Glue the wings to the back of the angel.

Angel Pie

Crust

- ★ 3 eggs, separated
- ★ 1/8 t. cream of tartar
- ★ 3/4 c. sugar

Filling

- ★ 1/2 c. sugar
- ★ 1 T. grated lemon peel
- ★ 3 T. lemon juice
- ★ 3 reserved egg yolks
- ★ 1 c. whipping cream, whipped

Preheat oven to 275° F. Grease a 9-inch pie plate.

In a small bowl, beat the egg whites with cream of tarter until frothy. Gradually add 3/4 c. sugar, beating continuously until stiff peaks form. Spread meringue over the bottom and sides of the prepared pie plate. The meringue will puff up during baking, so spread only to the top edge of the plate. Bake for 60 minutes. Turn off the oven, keep the door closed, and leave the crust inside to cool and dry.

In small saucepan, combine remaining ingredients except whipped cream. Cook over low heat, stirring constantly, until filling thickens. Allow to cool completely. Fold whipped cream into filling. Pour into meringue shell. Refrigerate overnight. If desired, garnish pie with thin lemon slices, grated lemon peel, or sugared lemon ribbons.

From heaven came
the angels bright
To shepherds watching in the
night. A newborn royal child, they
said, Lies yonder in a manger bed.

MARTIN LUTHER

In regions where there is snow,
children make snow angels.
They do this by lying flat in the snow and moving their legs back
and forth and their arms up and down (keeping knees and elbows
straight) at the same time. Then, they carefully stand up. The pattern
left in the snow looks like an angel's wings and robe.

From Heaven Above to Earth I Come

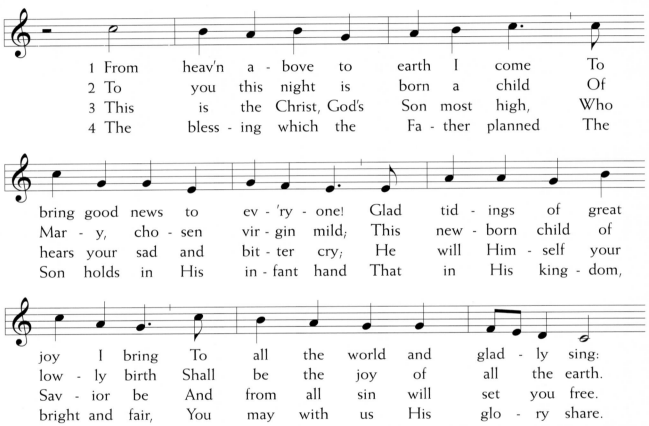

1 From heav'n a-bove to earth I come To
bring good news to ev-'ry-one! Glad tid-ings of great
joy I bring To all the world and glad-ly sing:

2 To you this night is born a child Of
Mar-y, cho-sen vir-gin mild; This new-born child of
low-ly birth Shall be the joy of all the earth.

3 This is the Christ, God's Son most high, Who
hears your sad and bit-ter cry; He will Him-self your
Sav-ior be And from all sin will set you free.

4 The bless-ing which the Fa-ther planned The
Son holds in His in-fant hand That in His king-dom,
bright and fair, You may with us His glo-ry share.

5 These are the signs which you will see
To let you know that it is He:
In manger bed, in swaddling clothes
The child who all the earth upholds.

6 How glad we'll be to find it so!
Then with the shepherds let us go
To see what God for us has done
In sending us His own dear Son.

7 Look, look, dear friends, look over there!
What lies within that manger bare?
Who is that lovely little one?
The baby Jesus, God's dear Son.

Martin Luther

wrote this 14-verse hymn in 1531 for his five-year-old son, Hans. It became part of the annual Christmas Eve festivities in the Luther home, where music was an important part of their everyday lives as well as part of their worship on Sundays and religious holidays. In the Luther family tradition, a man dressed as an angel would sing the opening verses. The children would respond by singing the verses following.

Text: Martin Luther, 1483–1546; tr. *Lutheran Book of Worship*, 1978

Welcome to Earth, O Noble Guest

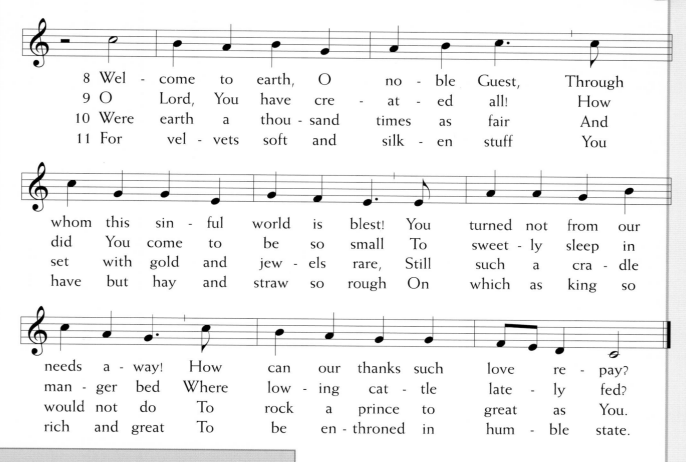

8 Wel - come to earth, O no - ble Guest, Through
9 O Lord, You have cre - at - ed all! How
10 Were earth a thou - sand times as fair And
11 For vel - vets soft and silk - en stuff You

whom this sin - ful world is blest! You turned not from our
did You come to be so small To sweet - ly sleep in
set with gold and jew - els rare, Still such a cra - dle
have but hay and straw so rough On which as king so

needs a - way! How can our thanks such love re - pay?
man - ger bed Where low - ing cat - tle late - ly fed?
would not do To rock a prince to great as You.
rich and great To be en - throned in hum - ble state.

12 O dearest Jesus, holy child,
Prepare a bed, soft, undefiled,
A holy shrine, within my heart,
That You and I need never part.

13 My heart for very joy now leaps;
My voice no longer silence keeps;
I too must join the angel throng
To sing with joy His cradlesong;

14 "Glory to God in highest heav'n,
Who unto us His Son has giv'n."
With angels sing in pious mirth:
A glad new year to all the earth!

O Little Town of Bethlehem

The night the world changed began like any other night. The shepherds would have herded their sheep into a protected bunch. Some would sleep. Some would keep watch. They might have talked about how much their flock would bring on the market or where they would lead them the next day. They might have talked about their families or the new Roman tax. Maybe they didn't talk at all. Perhaps in the distance they could see Bethlehem.

Bethlehem would be busy, of course. The ancient town was crowded with travelers who had come to register for the census ordered by Caesar Augustus. But on the hills above the town, it would have been quiet and still and dark.

"And an angel of the Lord appeared to them, and the glory of the Lord shone around them, and they were filled with fear" (Luke 2:9).

We can try to imagine it, but we don't really know what it was like to see and hear God's messenger, the angel, in all its heavenly glory.

We do know, however, that the Lord God chose the lowest class of people to hear the highest of announcements. And we know that the world had been waiting for thousands of years for this news that God's promise of a Savior was fulfilled. That "the hopes and fears of all the years" were finally, finally met with God's peace and grace.

Phillips Brooks came close to capturing the feeling of that first Christmas night when he visited the Holy Land in 1865. While his own land was being torn apart by a bitter civil war, this American minister experienced the majesty and awe of the land where Christ was born. The story goes that Brooks visited the Church of the Nativity in Bethlehem on Christmas Eve that year. And several years later, when he wanted a new Christmas hymn for his congregation, he recalled that night and wrote "O Little Town of Bethlehem." It remains a favorite of those who marvel at God's great gift.

O Little Town of Bethlehem

1 O little town of Bethlehem, How still we see thee lie!
2 For Christ is born of Mary, And, gathered all above
3 How silently, how silently, The wondrous gift is giv'n!
4 O holy Child of Bethlehem, Descend to us, we pray;

Above thy deep And dreamless sleep The silent stars go by;
While mortals sleep, The angels keep Their watch of wond'ring love.
So God imparts To human hearts The blessings of His heav'n.
Cast out our sin And enter in, Be born in us today.

Yet in thy dark streets shineth The everlasting light.
O morning stars, together Proclaim the holy birth,
No ear may hear His coming; But in this world of sin,
We hear the Christmas angels The great glad tidings tell;

The hopes and fears Of all the years Are met in thee tonight.
And praises sing To God the King, And peace to all the earth!
Where meek souls will Receive Him, still The dear Christ enters in.
Oh, come to us, Abide with us, Our Lord Immanuel!

Text: Phillips Brooks, 1835–93, ab.
Tune: ST. LOUIS, Lewis H. Redner, 1831–1908

Oh, Come, Little Children

"Let the children come to Me; do not hinder them, for to such belongs the kingdom of God" (Mark 10:14).

The shepherds came. The Wise Men came. The sick, the lame, the hurting came. And the children came. They came to Jesus, God in the flesh, who Himself came to us to bring forgiveness and peace.

This hymn was written in the mid-1800s by German author Christoph von Schmidt to teach children about the real gifts of Christmas. The composer, Johann Schulz, was just fifteen when he began his career as a musician. A classic Christmas hymn, it is most often sung by children as a processional or at the beginning of the service.

Let the children come!

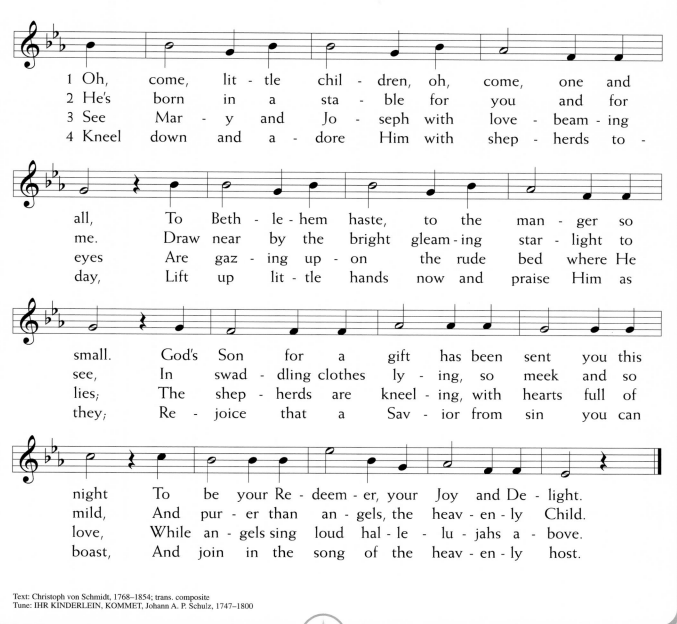

1 Oh, come, little children, oh, come, one and
2 He's born in a sta - ble for you and for
3 See Mar - y and Jo - seph with love - beam - ing
4 Kneel down and a - dore Him with shep - herds to -

all, To Beth - le - hem haste, to the man - ger so
me. Draw near by the bright gleam - ing star - light to
eyes Are gaz - ing up - on the rude bed where He
day, Lift up lit - tle hands now and praise Him as

small. God's Son for a gift has been sent you this
see, In swad - dling clothes ly - ing, so meek and so
lies; The shep - herds are kneel - ing, with hearts full of
they; Re - joice that a Sav - ior from sin you can

night To be your Re - deem - er, your Joy and De - light.
mild, And pur - er than an - gels, the heav - en - ly Child.
love, While an - gels sing loud hal - le - lu - jahs a - bove.
boast, And join in the song of the heav - en - ly host.

Text: Christoph von Schmidt, 1768–1854; trans. composite
Tune: IHR KINDERLEIN, KOMMET, Johann A. P. Schulz, 1747–1800

Oh, Come, All Ye Faithful

Do you ever get the feeling that your child is confused at Christmas? There is such a mixture of Santa, presents, parties, and fantasy. What are we really celebrating, and why?

It's important to remember the real story of the first Christmas and the love of God behind it. Our heavenly Father sent us a Savior who did not shrink from being poor and unrecognized. Christ wasn't even born in a house. We often forget this and tend to romanticize the manger in the stable. Mary and Joseph had a hard time of it. The shepherds who welcomed the Christ Child were the nobodies of society. Our God chooses hard and strange ways to win back His children. This is why Jesus came. He saves us from the power of sin, death, and devil and brings God's life back to us.

This is the Good News, and really the only reason we celebrate Christmas. See the heart of Christmas. Make Christmas come alive by centering the season in the birth of our Lord and Savior, Jesus Christ. And let us come and adore Christ the Lord.

FROM *THE BABY BORN IN A STABLE*

1 Oh, come, all ye faith-ful, Joy-ful and tri-um-phant! Oh,
2 High-est, most ho-ly, Light of light e-ter-nal,
3 Sing, choirs of an-gels, Sing in ex-ul-ta-tion,
4 Yea, Lord, we greet Thee, Born this hap-py morn-ing;

come ye, oh, come ye to Beth-le-hem;
Born of a vir-gin, a mor-tal He comes;
Sing, all ye cit-i-zens of heav-en a-bove!
Je-sus, to Thee be glo-ry giv'n!

Come and be-hold Him Born the King of an-gels:
Son of the Fa-ther Now in flesh ap-pear-ing!
Glo-ry to God In the high-est:
Word of the Fa-ther, Now in flesh ap-pear-ing!

Refrain
Oh, come, let us a-dore Him, Oh, come, let us a-dore Him,

Oh, come, let us a-dore Him, Christ the Lord!

Text: attr. John F. Wade, c. 1711–86; tr. composite
Tune: ADESTE FIDELES, John F. Wade, c. 1711–86

He Whom Shepherds Once Came Praising

And it came to pass, as the angels were gone away from them into heaven, the shepherds said one to another, Let us now go even unto Bethlehem, and see this thing which is come to pass, which the Lord hath made known unto us. And they came with haste, and found Mary, and Joseph, and the babe lying in a manger. And when they had seen *it*, they made known abroad the saying which was told them concerning this child.

And all they that heard *it* wondered at those things which were told them by the shepherds. But Mary kept all these things, and pondered *them* in her heart.

And the shepherds returned, glorifying and praising God for all the things that they had heard and seen, as it was told unto them.

LUKE 2:15–20 KJV

Of the shepherds we are told that after they found the newborn King and worshiped Him, "they made known abroad the saying which was told them concerning this child."

That was how they served the infant King. They became missionaries at once, telling their friends and neighbors of the things they saw and heard.

FROM *LET US NOW GO EVEN UNTO BETHLEHEM*

26

This traditional German carol was written in the 1300s to symbolize the announcement of Christ's birth to the four corners of the world. A responsive carol, it is customarily sung by choirs and the congregation. Four children's choirs stand in the four corners of the church. Singing a capella, the first choir sings the first line of the *Quem pastores*. The second choir sings the second line, and so on. Then, a choir of adults sings the first stanza of the *Nunc angelorum*. Accompanied, the congregation joins the choirs in the refrain, the *Resonet in laudibus*. The rest of the hymn verses are sung the same way.

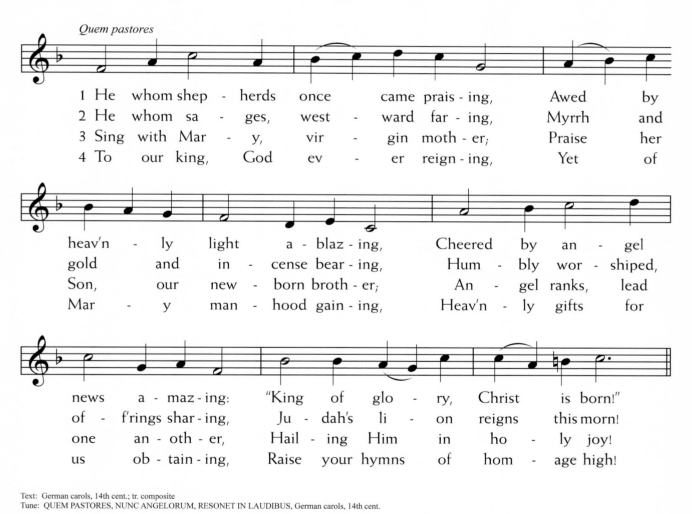

Quem pastores

1 He whom shep - herds once came prais - ing, Awed by
2 He whom sa - ges, west - ward far - ing, Myrrh and
3 Sing with Mar - y, vir - gin moth - er; Praise her
4 To our king, God ev - er reign - ing, Yet of

heav'n - ly light a - blaz - ing, Cheered by an - gel
gold and in - cense bear - ing, Hum - bly wor - shiped,
Son, our new - born broth - er; An - gel ranks, lead
Mar - y man - hood gain - ing, Heav'n - ly gifts for

news a - maz - ing: "King of glo - ry, Christ is born!"
of - f'rings shar - ing, Ju - dah's li - on reigns this morn!
one an - oth - er, Hail - ing Him in ho - ly joy!
us ob - tain - ing, Raise your hymns of hom - age high!

Text: German carols, 14th cent.; tr. composite
Tune: QUEM PASTORES, NUNC ANGELORUM, RESONET IN LAUDIBUS, German carols, 14th cent.

Nunc angelorum

The glo- rious an - gels came to- day, A - glow with light in -
"God's maj - es - ty has come to earth And sent His on - ly
Then sang the an - gels this re- frain: "To God on high a -
The won- d'ring shep - herds said: "Be- hold! Let us now go with

to the night of dark - ness deep, To shep- herds who by
Son to you in hu - man- kind; A cho - sen vir - gin
lone give praise and glo - ry, And peace on earth a -
all good speed to Beth - le - hem To see this thing the

moon's bright ray Did in the field o'er sheep their si - lent
gave Him birth. In Da - vid's town the ho - ly in - fant
gain shall reign. Let all on earth with glad - ness heed this
Lord has told; The sheep are safe; He will in - deed take

vig - il keep. "Joy, great joy and tid - ings glad we
you will find, Ly - ing help - less in a man - ger,
sto - ry And re - joice in His good- will." The
care of them." There they found the won - der child, in

28

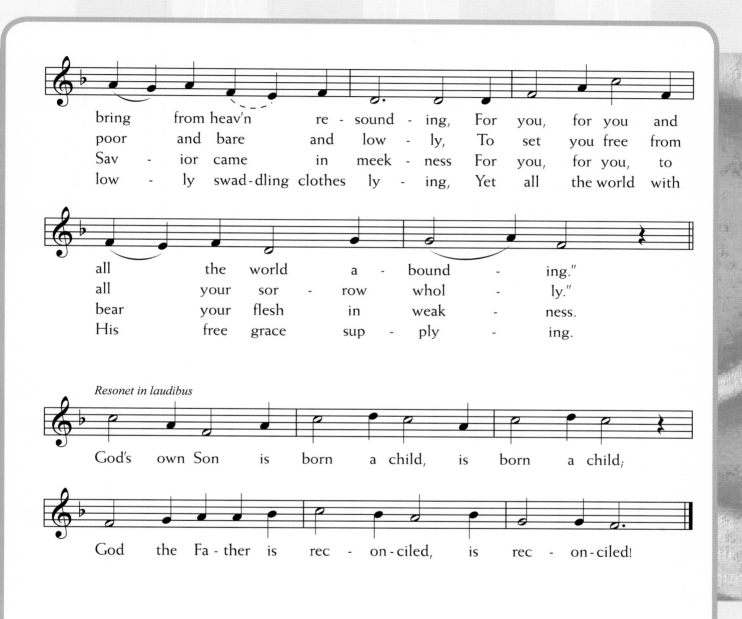

bring from heav'n re - sound - ing, For you, for you and
poor and bare and low - ly, To set you free from
Sav - ior came in meek - ness For you, for you, to
low - ly swad-dling clothes ly - ing, Yet all the world with

all the world a - bound - ing."
all your sor - row whol - ly."
bear your flesh in weak - ness.
His free grace sup - ply - ing.

Resonet in laudibus

God's own Son is born a child, is born a child;

God the Fa - ther is rec - on - ciled, is rec - on - ciled!

Away in a Manger

For to us a child is born,
to us a son is given,
and the government shall be
upon His shoulder,
and His name shall be called
Wonderful Counselor, Mighty God,
Everlasting Father, Prince of Peace.

ISAIAH 9:6

Wake Up, Brother, Listen

Wake up, brother, listen to the wondrous news,
What at midnight startled all our lambs and ewes.
They had just come in from grazing
And lay down when the amazing
    light appeared,
And a sound from heaven woke them,
    strange and feared.
Come to Bethl'em, come now, to the blessed site,
We shall see what happened there this very night,
Just to spend a little while there,
And to see the precious Child there,
    in the hay,
Wrapped in swaddling garments,
    as the angels say.

JAROSLAV VAJDA

On a Silent Night

The story of our Savior's birth can never be told too many times. It draws children in with its wonderful and delightful images. There is action. There is drama. There is the bond of a personal message of God's love made real through a tiny baby.

To make it more real, engage your child in the story. Read a Christmas storybook with your child. Sing your favorite carol and talk about how you enjoy singing about Jesus' birth. Assure your little one that the light of God's love shines on her and through her. And think about the miracle of God's love that happened on a silent night. Our Savior, born so long ago, died and rose for our salvation. His love still shines today!

1 A - way in a man - ger, no crib for a bed, The
2 The cat - tle are low - ing, the Ba - by a - wakes, But
3 Be near me, Lord Je - sus; I ask Thee to stay Close

lit - tle Lord Je - sus laid down His sweet head. The
lit - tle Lord Je - sus, no cry - ing He makes. I
by me for - ev - er and love me, I pray. Bless

stars in the bright sky looked down where He lay, The
love Thee, Lord Je - sus! Look down from the sky, And
all the dear chil - dren in Thy ten - der care, And

lit - tle Lord Je - sus a - sleep on the hay.
stay by my side un - til morn - ing is nigh.
take us to heav - en to live with Thee there.

Text: Author unknown, c. 1883, sts. 1–2; John T. McFarland, 1851–1913, st. 3, alt.
Tune: CRADLE SONG, William J. Kirkpatrick, 1838–1921

Change the Emphasis

How do you fight the pull to do more, buy more, celebrate more? Just when it seems that consumerism is pandemic, these busy days provide the perfect opportunity to be deliberate about living in the world but not of the world, to focus on the Christ in Christmas. Simplifying Christmas is manageable, but requires a little forethought. Here are some ideas to get you started:

- On December 6—St. Nicholas's Day—fill children's shoes with gold foil-covered chocolate coins. Read a St. Nicholas story. Then put away the Santa stuff and focus on Jesus' birthday the rest of the month.

- Have your whole family participate in your church or community's living Nativity. Take a picture and hang it on your Christmas tree or send it in cards.

- Go caroling—neighbors, shut-ins, nursing home residents receive immeasurable pleasure from a personal visit and Christmas message.

- Set up a crèche, but don't include the Jesus or Wise Men figures. As the family goes to bed on Christmas Eve, have the youngest child place the Jesus figure in its proper spot. Then, on Epiphany, have the oldest child add the Wise Men.

- Attend Advent and worship services as a family. If your church celebrates with a candlelight service on Christmas Eve, bundle little ones in their pj's rather than uncomfortable Christmas finery.

- Give anonymous gifts. Bishop Nicholas, the original Sinter Clausen, was legendary for his anonymous gifts. Often when a person receives an anonymous present, Jesus gets the credit. You also might share with your child that giving to another person in Jesus' name is like giving a gift to Jesus.

- Stack gifts under the tree by giver rather than receiver. Take turns giving each gift to recipients.

- At Christmas dinner, place a crèche figure on each plate. Invite each diner to tell what that person gave the Christ Child. For example, Joseph gave Jesus a soft, clean bed. The shepherds gave Jesus honor as they knelt before Him.

Little Baby in the Cradle

Little Baby in the cradle,
Angels brought the news to earth,
When they told the lowly shepherds
All about the wondrous birth.

Little Baby in the cradle,
Shepherds once rejoiced to see
Such a tiny little baby,
As they prayed on bended knee.

Little Baby in the cradle,
We are happy, too, today,
And like the lowly shepherds
We have come to kneel and pray.

Little Baby in the cradle,
Wise Men saw the shining star,
And they followed, bringing with them
Precious presents from afar.

Little Baby in the cradle,
We have little gifts to bring,
Take our hearts and hands and voices;
Of You now we, too, would sing.

Little Baby in the cradle,
Come into our hearts, we pray;
Let them be your holy temple.
Come to us on Christmas Day.

From *The Real Meaning of Christmas*

In the thirteenth century,

Francis of Assisi started the Christmas custom of a crèche. A crèche is a scene showing the manger and the stable where Jesus was born. It reminds us how God the Son came into the world as a baby to be our Savior. Jesus left heaven and became poor so we could go to heaven and share its riches.

The crèche reminds us that Jesus came to be the Savior of all people. Although Jesus was born in a barn as a little baby, He is King of kings and the true God.

Baby Jesus, God's own Son,

(point to heaven)

Surely loves us, ev'ry one.

(point to self)

There He lies, asleep on hay;

(point to manger)

Let Him come to you today.

(point to others)

From *Signs and Symbols of Christmas*

In a Little Stable

We've a Story to Tell

In a field near Bethlehem town
Some shepherds watched their sheep.
The night was dark and quiet.
Most people were asleep.

But then an angel came and said,
"The Savior, Christ, is born.
You'll find Him in a manger bed
This early Christmas morn."

The sky now filled with angels
Singing praises to God in heaven.
After they left, the shepherds looked
For the Savior God had given.

They found Him as the angel said.
The story was really true.
The shepherds believed the story
And we believe it too!

There's more to the story.
Some Wise Men saw the star of Jesus' birth.
They said, "Let's go find the Baby.
He's King of all the earth."

And so, these men—some call them kings—
Traveled a long, long way
To worship the young Child, Jesus,
Who came the world to save.

They brought rich gifts of myrrh
And frankincense and gold
To show their love for the Savior
First promised to people of old.

But what of today?
Is the story still true?
Yes! Jesus was born
For me. And for you.

FROM *WE'VE A STORY TO TELL*

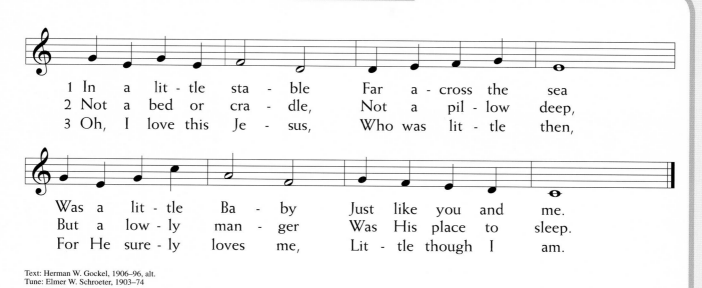

Text: Herman W. Gockel, 1906–96, alt.
Tune: Elmer W. Schroeter, 1903–74

Infant Holy, Infant Lowly

Angels were the first to sing of Christmas joy.

That holy night they lit the sky over the fields of Bethlehem! Their audience? Not kings or wealthy merchants, but shepherds—humble shepherds!

> And in the same region there were shepherds out in the field, keeping watch over their flock by night. And an angel of the Lord appeared to them, and the glory of the Lord shone around them, and they were filled with fear. And the angel said to them, "Fear not, for behold, I bring you good news of a great joy that will be for all the people. For unto you is born this day in the city of David a Savior, who is Christ the Lord." (Luke 2:8–11)

The angel told the shepherds where to find the Baby. In a manger, they said, in swaddling cloths.

Then suddenly a thousand, thousand angels filled the night sky! Wouldn't it have been something to have been there? Imagine it … a choir of angels!

Now, if you were a shepherd out in your field and an angel came and told you where to find the Savior of the world, what would you do? You'd run as quickly as you could to see Him! That's exactly what they did.

> The shepherds said to one another, "Let us go over to Bethlehem and see this thing that has happened, which the Lord has made known to us." And they went with haste and found Mary and Joseph, and the Baby lying in a manger. (Luke 2:15–16)

The shepherds were the first to hear the news and see the Child. They sang for joy at the news, "glorifying and praising God for all they had heard and seen, as it had been told them" (Luke 2:20).

We Christians sing of promise, love, and joy. It's Christmas now. Sing out loud and strong our Gospel song! Sing of Christmas!

FROM *Children Sing of Christmas*

1 In - fant ho - ly, in - fant low - ly, For His bed a cat - tle stall;
2 Flocks were sleep - ing, shep - herds keep - ing Vig - il till the morn - ing new

Ox - en low - ing, lit - tle know - ing Christ the child is Lord of all.
Saw the glo - ry, heard the sto - ry, Tid - ings of a Gos - pel true.

Swift - ly wing - ing, an - gels sing - ing, Bells are ring - ing, tid - ings bring - ing:
Thus re - joic - ing, free from sor - row, Prais - es voic - ing, greet the mor - row:

Christ the child is Lord of all! Christ the child is Lord of all!
Christ the child was born for you! Christ the child was born for you!

Text: Polish carol; tr. Edith M. G. Reed, 1885–1933, alt.
Tune: W ZLOBIE LEZY, Polish carol

Now Sing We, Now Rejoice

Carols and Hymns

What's the difference? Hymns convey a spiritual truth, grounded in Scripture. They express a specific belief, such as a biblical truth about God or His work in our lives as Christians. More formal by design, hymns are often poetry with regular meter. They are intended to be sung in church by the congregation. Hymns can be traced to the psalmists.

Carols also typically express a Christian belief or biblical truth, but are much more casually written and sung than hymns. Defined as "a song of joy, exultation, or mirth," carols can even be considered to be folksongs. Dating to the early thirteenth century, they are traditionally sung in the streets by people strolling or dancing. "I Saw Three Ships" is thought to be the first genuine Christmas carol.

Much is said about "peace" these days, but much of what is said and written has nothing to do with the peace of which the angels sang on that first Christmas night in Bethlehem. The "peace on earth" the angels sang about was not the peace of man to man. It was, above all else, peace between God and man—the peace of reconciliation.

"Peace on earth and mercy mild, God and sinners reconciled!" It was the peace of soul, peace of mind, peace of conscience that comes from the knowledge that God was in Christ—in that little Babe of Bethlehem— "reconciling the world to Himself, not counting their trespasses against them" (2 Corinthians. 5:19). It was the peace of which the apostle later spoke when he said, "Therefore, since we have been justified by faith, we have peace with God through our Lord Jesus Christ" (Romans 5:1).

This heavenly peace, this "peace of God, which surpasses all understanding (Philippians 4:7)," is given fully and freely to all who kneel in humble faith at Bethlehem's manger and acknowledge the infant Savior as their Lord and King.

May God bless us and favor us all with a happy Christmas season and may He grant that we shall experience the indescribable peace of those who have found forgiveness at the manger of the Christ Child.

FROM ON EARTH PEACE

1 Now sing we, now re-joice With heart and soul and voice.
2 God's Son, come from a-bove, Your grace and sav-ing love
3 We see God's love di-vine For us in Je-sus shine.
4 Where is that place so fair? Oh, no-where else but there

Life's most pre-cious trea-sure Here poor in man-ger lies;
To my spir-it bring-ing, O pure and ho-ly Child,
Guilt of sin had taught us But death and mis-er-y;
Where the an-gel voic-es With God's re-deemed u-nite,

He brings pur-er plea-sure Than sun-light from the skies.
Fill my heart with sing-ing For grace so great and mild.
Then our Ran-som bought us God's bright e-ter-ni-ty.
Awed that He re-joic-es To share His joy and light.

Christ is born to-day! Christ is born to-day!
Draw me, Lord, to You! Draw me, Lord, to You!
Oh, that we were there! Oh, that we were there!
Oh, that we were there! Oh, that we were there!

Text: medieval Latin hymn; tr. F. Samuel Janzow, 1913–2001
Tune: IN DULCI JUBILO, German carol, 14th cent.

Silent Night, Holy Night

Silent night, holy night; all is calm and bright. But was it really a silent, calm place?

No, it was not. It was a world much like ours today. It was a world noisy with the hustle and bustle of people trying to get ahead. It was a world nervous about wars and rebellions. It was a world facing a new tax by the Romans, which came on top of too many existing taxes.

This world was turned upside down by a decree from Caesar that forced people to travel to other parts of the country. Everyone had to enter his name on the tax rolls in the home of his ancient ancestors. No one was given an exemption, not even expectant mothers. Just to be sure nothing and no one got in the way of this tax program, soldiers of Rome were ready to enforce the law. These soldiers were always present because there was always the threat of rebellion against Rome.

In the middle of all this trouble and turmoil, God made a quiet place, a place to send His Son. Here was that silent place where God entered the world unnoticed.

There was no publicity, no commotion. There was only God and Mary, away from the noisy world but really in the very center of it. And there was the Child, who had no father on earth and no mother in heaven. …

In the middle of a troubled world, God made a quiet place and a silent night to send us His Son. This is the way God so often does things, in silence and in secret.

There was a worship service that night, a service for a congregation of humble, faithful men. God worked through them to spread the good news of His plan for man's salvation.

What is it we want for Christmas? Is it the gaiety, noise, and excitement of a party? Is it the feverish getting and giving of gifts? Is it familiar carols and heightened spirits that come naturally with the season?

Yes, we want these things, and much more. We want the Child of Bethlehem—but also the Christ of Calvary, the open tomb, and the Mount of Ascension, for we know we cannot have the one without the others.

Therefore may we always journey to His manger, kneel with the shepherds, and adore with the Magi. May we always remember that unto *us* is born a Savior!

FROM *UNTO US A SAVIOR*

1 Si - lent night, ho - ly night! All is calm,
2 Si - lent night, ho - ly night! Shep - herds quake
3 Si - lent night, ho - ly night! Son of God,

all is bright Round yon vir - gin moth - er and child.
at the sight; Glo - ries stream from heav - en a - far,
love's pure light Ra - diant beams from Your ho-ly face

Ho - ly in - fant, so ten - der and mild, Sleep in heav - en - ly
Heav'n - ly hosts sing, Al - le - lu - ia! Christ, the Sav - ior, is
With the dawn of re - deem - ing grace, Je - sus, Lord, at Your

peace, Sleep in heav - en - ly peace.
born! Christ, the Sav - ior, is born!
birth, Je - sus, Lord, at Your birth.

Text: Joseph Mohr, 1792–1848; tr. John F. Young, 1820–85
Tune: STILLE NACHT, Franz Gruber, 1787–1863

On a Silent Night

On a silent night
Came the soft moonlight,
With beauty the town to adorn.

'Twas a time so dear
With the heavens near,
When the Bethlehem Child was born.

For our God above
Sent His Son in love
To a world so lonely and lost.

And the angels told,
In the sky aglow,
How He came, not counting the cost.

The shepherds were there
In the cold night air.
They were awed to see such a sight:

The mother so mild
With her precious Child
On that glad and glorious night!

Then Wise Men of old
Heard the story told,
How a star would be shining bright.

It would show the way
Where the Christ Child lay,
Surrounded by God's very light!

Now the baby sleeps
While His mother keeps
Many loving thoughts in her heart:

For as God's Son He'll claim
Our sin with its stain,
And salvation to us He'll impart.

And her heart knows well
That the years will tell
How He saved us all with His love.

And she knows we will sing
Of her newborn King
On earth and in heaven above!

Lord, it's been so long
Since the angels' song,
But still the bright star points to Thee.

And now I well know
That its golden glow
Says the star still shines for me!

FROM *ON A SILENT NIGHT*

Snowy Snacks

- ⭐ **Flour tortillas**
- ⭐ **Scissors**
- ⭐ **Powered sugar**
- ⭐ **Nonstick skillet**
- ⭐ **Cooking spray**

Fold tortilla into quarters, but don't crease or tear it. With the scissors, cut away parts of the tortilla. Unfold tortilla.

Spray skillet with cooking spray and heat over medium heat. Fry tortilla, one side at a time, until it's brown and crispy.

Dredge with powdered sugar and enjoy!

Silent Night Ornaments

- ⭐ **Clear glass ornaments (found at craft and discount stores)**
- ⭐ **Decorative items for filling the ornaments, such as tinsel, craft gel crystals, glitter, imitation snow, craft paint, etc.**
- ⭐ **Craft glue**
- ⭐ **Ornament hangers or ribbon**

Remove the metal top and carefully fill each ornament with a decorative item suggested above. For example, pour a small amount of metallic craft paint and swirl inside the ornament. Pour out excess paint. Allow paint to dry for several minutes. Add a small amount of glitter and shake vigorously.

If desired, use craft paint pens to decorate the outside of the ornament, adding appropriate words such as "Silent Night, Holy Night," "Joy," or "Peace."

Use a hanger or ribbon to hang the ornaments on your tree.

Once in Royal David's City

Bethlehem, which means "house of bread," is rich in biblical history. Located about six miles south of Jerusalem, Bethlehem is where Jacob buried his wife Rachel (Genesis 35:16–20). In the area of Bethlehem, Ruth gleaned grain in the fields of Boaz (Ruth 2:1–12). Bethlehem was the hometown of Jesse and his family. It was the place where David, great-grandson of Ruth, was anointed by Samuel to be king (1 Samuel 16:1–13).

"Once in royal David's city," the Bread of Life, Jesus, was born. Bethlehem had not really changed—it was still a sleepy village caught in the busyness of people counters, an overfilled inn, and shepherds watching their sheep on the suburban hills. But sleepy Bethlehem was awakened by a host of angels singing about the birth of the Savior.

All of this was part of God's plan to have the greater son of David, Jesus, the Bread of Life, born for us. The Bread of Life born at the House of Bread, Bethlehem, nourishes our lives of faith with His Word and His body and blood given for the forgiveness of our sin. Such great things from such a small place.

FROM *EMMANUEL, GOD WITH US!*

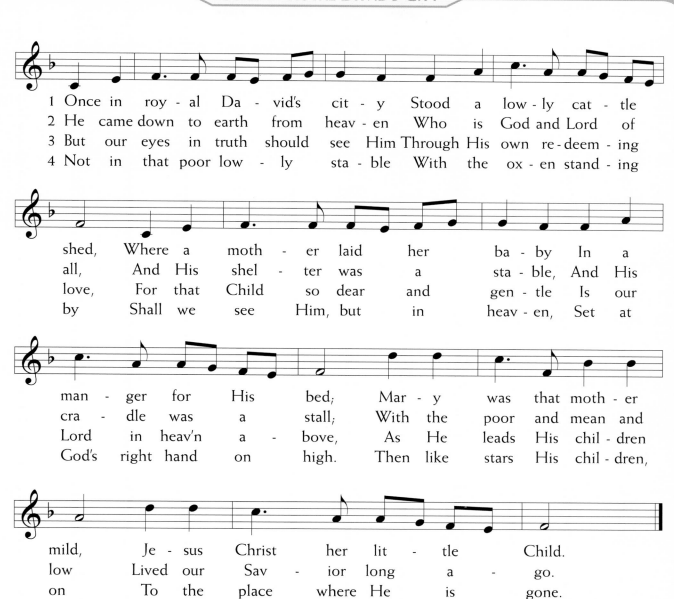

1 Once in roy - al Da - vid's cit - y Stood a low - ly cat - tle
2 He came down to earth from heav - en Who is God and Lord of
3 But our eyes in truth should see Him Through His own re - deem - ing
4 Not in that poor low - ly sta - ble With the ox - en stand - ing

shed, Where a moth - er laid her ba - by In a
all, And His shel - ter was a sta - ble, And His
love, For that Child so dear and gen - tle Is our
by Shall we see Him, but in heav - en, Set at

man - ger for His bed; Mar - y was that moth - er
cra - dle was a stall; With the poor and mean and
Lord in heav'n a - bove, As He leads His chil - dren
God's right hand on high. Then like stars His chil - dren,

mild, Je - sus Christ her lit - tle Child.
low Lived our Sav - ior long a - go.
on To the place where He is gone.
crowned, All in white, His praise will sound!

Text: Cecil Frances Alexander, 1823–95, alt.
Tune: IRBY, Henry J. Gauntlett, 1805–76

But you, O Bethlehem

Ephrathah, who are too little to be
among the clans of Judah, from you
shall come forth for Me one who is to
be ruler in Israel, whose coming forth is
from of old, from ancient days.

MICAH 5:2

Once in royal David's city

Stood a lowly cattle shed,
Where a mother laid her baby
In a manger for His bed;
Mary was that mother mild,
Jesus Christ her little child.

LSB 376:1

During these Christmas days,
our thoughts easily turn to consider the little
town where mother Mary gave birth to our
Savior. The story of that ancient and sacred
village engages us still today. Before its gates
Jacob buried his beloved Rachel (Genesis 35).
In the fields of Bethlehem pious and faithful
Ruth gleaned and gathered her sheaves for her
master Boaz (Ruth). On the hillsides above,
her great-grandson David tended his father's
flocks. The brook from which he so longed to
drink in his great thirst (2 Samuel 23:15) still
murmurs in the green valley at the foot of the
town. To the little town of Bethlehem came
Joseph and his young wife when great David's
greater Son was born in a lowly cattle shed.

How wonderful are the ways of God! The
Ruler of Israel, the everlasting King of mercy,
the Lord of peace is not born in some lordly
mansion in Athens or in an imperial palace
in Rome, but in the poor, little hill village,

insignificant Bethlehem. But our God and Father in heaven always does this: a virgin with child; a faithful husband with the proper bloodlines; an enforced journey; choirs of heavenly hosts sing the great Good News to society's lowliest members, the shepherds. "He has shown strength with His arm; He has scattered the proud in the thoughts of their hearts; He has brought down the mighty from their thrones and exalted those of humble estate" (Luke 1:51–52).

King David no longer sat on his throne and his hometown was nearly forgotten in the Judean landscape. Yet the promise of salvation was not forgotten. "And our eyes at last shall see Him, Through His own redeeming love; For that child so dear and gentle Is our Lord in heav'n above" (*LSB* 376:4). And lowly Bethlehem, poor and forgotten Bethlehem, is exalted and becomes again the hometown of Israel's King, the long-expected King—Jesus Christ!

Scot Kinnaman

O holy Child of Bethlehem,

Descend to us, we pray;
Cast out our sin, and enter in,
Be born in us today.
We hear the Christmas angels
The great glad tidings tell;
Oh, come to us, abide with us,
Our Lord Immanuel!

LSB 361:4

Christmas isn't only A decorated tree,

Holly wreaths and evergreen,
And gifts for you and me.

Christmas is remembering
A night so long ago,
A little town called Bethlehem,
A manger bed so low.

Christmas is remembering
The Baby on the hay.
That little one is God's own Son,
Our Savior, born that day.

Christmas is remembering
Why He came down to earth,
Why God gave us His only Son,
The reason for Christ's birth.

Christmas is remembering
The cross on which He died
For you, for me, for all of us;
Christ Jesus crucified!

FROM *Come, Lord Jesus*

Sweetest Song of This Bright Season

Sweetest song of this bright season
Is the one glad hearts compose:
Jesus is the joy and reason
For the peace His birth bestows;
So, all children sing and say:
Peace and joy! It's Christmas Day!

HECTOR HOPPE

Come, children all, with one accord

Your grateful praises sing;
This is the birthday of our Lord,
Your Savior and your king.

Come, see the manger-cradle Child
Upon His mother's arm;
The heavenly Father watcheth o'er
And keepeth them from harm.

O hark, the sweet-voiced angels sing,
Rejoicing in His birth,
"Glory to God, good will to men,
And peace o'er all the earth."

Now let our voices join the song
To celebrate His birth,
The Child of God's great heart of love,
The gift of heaven to earth.

FROM *On Earth Peace*

Adults: Lit - tle chil - dren, can you tell, Do you know the
Children: Yes, we know the sto - ry well; Lis - ten now, and
For a lit - tle Babe that day Cra - dled in a

sto - ry well, Ev - 'ry girl and ev - 'ry boy, Why the an - gels
hear us tell, Ev - 'ry girl and ev - 'ry boy, Why the an - gels
man - ger lay, Born on earth our Lord to be; This the won - d'ring

sing for joy On the Christ - mas morn - ing?
sing for joy On the Christ - mas morn - ing.
an - gels see On the Christ - mas morn - ing.

Text: Unknown
Tune: Unknown

Joy to the World

The air is filled with the music of Christmas, and an overflowing joy wells from the hearts of Christians.

Christmas! How the Christian heart swells at the sound of the word! And why? Because man—blind, sinful, lost, and condemned man—was caught up in the arms of a gracious God who loved him with an everlasting love. On the one side there was man, "having no hope and without God in the world" (Ephesians 2:12), doomed to everlasting death. On the other side, there was God, "full of compassion, and gracious, longsuffering, and plenteous in mercy" (Psalm 86:15 KJV), who "so loved the world, that He gave His only Son" (John 3:16) for man's salvation. Now man can be a child of God by the grace God offers freely in His Son, "that whoever believes in Him should not perish but have eternal life" (John 3:16).

Oh, the blessed state of those who come with grateful and believing hearts to the manger of the Christ Child! Oh, the blessed festival of the Savior's birth, that helps us to look beyond the sins and troubles of this earth to the joys of heaven on the other side!

Away, then, all earthly care and sorrow! This is Christmas, when peace fills our hearts—abiding peace—because we are free from sin through our Lord and Savior Jesus Christ. And having peace, we have a full measure of joy, "pressed down, shaken together, running over" (Luke 6:38).

FROM *CHRISTMAS JOY*

1 Joy to the world, the Lord is come! Let earth re-
2 Joy to the earth, the Sav - ior reigns! Let all their
3 No more let sin and sor - row grow Nor thorns in -
4 He rules the world with truth and grace And makes the

ceive its King; Let ev - 'ry heart pre - pare Him
songs em - ploy While fields and floods, rocks, hills, and
fest the ground; He comes to make His bless - ings
na - tions prove The glo - ries of His righ - teous -

room And heav'n and na - ture sing, And heav'n and na - ture
plains Re - peat the sound - ing joy, Re - peat the sound - ing
flow Far as the curse is found, Far as the curse is
ness And won - ders of His love, And won - ders of His

sing, And heav'n, and heav'n and na - ture sing.
joy, Re - peat, re - peat the sound - ing joy.
found, Far as, far as the curse is found.
love, And won - ders, won - ders of His love.

Text: Isaac Watts, 1674–1748, alt.
Tune: ANTIOCH, George F. Handel, 1685–1759, adapt.

As with Gladness Men of Old

Ever Since the Savior Came

Ever since the Savior came
nothing is the same.
One day of all the days of earth,
one solitary promised birth,
one Name, and gloom is turned to mirth:
nothing is the same.

Ever since the Savior came
nothing is the same.
For shepherds calloused, tired, and bored,
whose spirits with the angels' soared,
who ran to worship Christ the Lord,
nothing was the same.

Ever since the Savior came
nothing is the same.
For learned sages, world-wise,
who searched for meaning in the skies,
and saw the Morning Star arise,
nothing was the same.

Ever since the Savior came
nothing is the same.
God's just demands are satisfied,
and death destroyed by One who died,
and Christmas ends in Eastertide:
nothing is the same.

Ever since we followed You
everything is new:
a love we never knew before,
a joy we never felt before,
a peace we never found before,
everything is new
everything is new!

Jaroslav Vajda

At the top of our lighted Christmas tree is a star.

Stars remind us of the great power and majesty of God. They make us look beyond our small world toward the infinity of heaven.

The five-pointed star is used on the Christmas tree to represent the figure of Christ, with a head, two outstretched arms, and two legs. Christ is the "bright and morning Star," who showed to us God's majesty and everlasting love.

Of course the star also reminds us of that star which led the Wise Men from the East to Jesus, as Saint Matthew wrote: "And, lo, the star, which they saw in the east, went before them, till it came and stood over where the young child was. When they saw the star, they rejoiced with exceeding great joy" (Matthew 2:9–10 KJV).

From *Signs and Symbols of Christmas*

1 As with glad-ness men of old Did the guid-ing star be-hold;
2 As with joy-ful steps they sped, Sav-ior, to Thy low-ly bed,
3 As they of-fered gifts most rare At Thy cra-dle, rude and bare,

4 Ho-ly Je-sus, ev-'ry day Keep us in the nar-row way;
5 In the heav'n-ly coun-try bright Need they no cre-a-ted light;

As with joy they hailed its light, Lead-ing on-ward, beam-ing bright;
There to bend the knee be-fore Thee, whom heav'n and earth a-dore;
So may we with ho-ly joy, Pure and free from sin's al-loy,

And when earth-ly things are past, Bring our ran-somed souls at last
Thou its light, its joy, its crown, Thou its sun which goes not down;

So, most gra-cious Lord, may we Ev-er-more be led by Thee.
So may we with will-ing feet Ev-er seek Thy mer-cy seat.
All our cost-liest trea-sures bring, Christ, to Thee, our heav'n-ly king.

Where they need no star to guide, Where no clouds Thy glo-ry hide.
There for-ev-er may we sing Al-le-lu-ias to our King.

Text: William C. Dix, 1837–98, alt.
Tune: DIX, Conrad Kocher, 1786–1872

What Child Is This?

The Visit of the Wise Men

The Wise Men—not members of God's people and living far away—would seem to be unlikely worshipers of the Christ Child. And yet, so eager were they to worship Him and bring Him gifts that they overcame countless difficulties, including the treachery of the king.

It would be a beautiful thing if we could catch more of that enthusiasm for worship and gift-bringing—and communicate it to our children. Our knowledge of what God in His overwhelming love has done for us in sending His Son into the world—reconciling sinful humanity to Himself through Jesus' atoning death—is so much greater than that of the Wise Men. And we certainly don't have to overcome the kind of obstacles they faced!

It has been said: "Wise men seek Him still." God grant us—and our children—such heavenly wisdom!

FROM *BECAUSE OF CHRISTMAS*

Lullaby for the Christ Child

Baby Jesus, sound asleep,
What strange lodgings here you keep.
Here where cattle make their home
You, the Son of God, have come.
Rock-a-bye in manger small,
Rock-a-bye the Lord of all.

Baby Jesus, children sing
Glorias to You, our King.
Shepherds leave behind their fear
And come for worship and good cheer.
Rock-a-bye in manger small,
Rock-a-bye the Lord of all.

FROM *BECAUSE OF CHRISTMAS*

1 What Child is this, who, laid to rest, On Mar - y's lap is sleep - ing? Whom an - gels greet with an - thems sweet While shep - herds watch are keep - ing? This, this is Christ the King, Whom shep - herds guard and an - gels sing; Haste, haste to bring Him laud, The Babe, the Son of Mar - y!

2 Why lies He in such mean es - tate Where ox and ass are feed - ing? Good Chris - tian, fear; for sin - ners here The si - lent Word is plead - ing. Nails, spear shall pierce Him through, The cross be borne for me, for you; Hail, hail the Word made flesh, The Babe, the Son of Mar - y!

3 So bring Him in - cense, gold, and myrrh; Come, peas - ant, king, to own Him. The King of kings sal - va - tion brings; Let lov - ing hearts en - throne Him. Raise, raise the song on high, The vir - gin sings her lul - la - by; Joy, joy, for Christ is born, The Babe, the Son of Mar - y!

Text: William C. Dix, 1837–98
Tune: GREENSLEEVES, English ballad, 16th cent.

Songs of Thankfulness and Praise

The Happiest Search

The Wise Men, the shepherds, and King Herod searched for the baby King for different reasons and with different results.

The Wise Men and the shepherds searched with faith in God's Word. By a bright new star and Scripture, God guided the Wise Men to the newborn King of the Jews. To the shepherds, God sent an angel to declare the good news that the long-promised Messiah had been born.

The Wise Men were the first Gentiles and the shepherds were the first Jews to find the Savior. They worshiped the Babe, God's Son, with hearts aglow with joy and praise. The Wise Men gave their precious treasures to the baby King, who was God's precious gift of love to them. The shepherds gave to the infant Jesus their lips, with which they told the glad message of His lowly but royal birth. For He was God's message of the forgiveness of sins to them.

But Herod, in his unbelief, planned to find and kill the infant King. Herod feared the loss of his wealth and power to the baby King, whose only thrones were a manger and a cross and whose royal robes were swaddling clothes and a seamless garment. Herod never found the Savior and in death lost his wealth, his power, and his soul.

From *The Happiest Search*

Scripture

Now when Jesus was born in Bethlehem of Judaea in the days of Herod the king, behold, there came wise men from the east to Jerusalem, Saying, Where is He that is born King of the Jews? for we have seen His star in the east, and are come to worship Him. (Matthew 2:1–2 KJV)

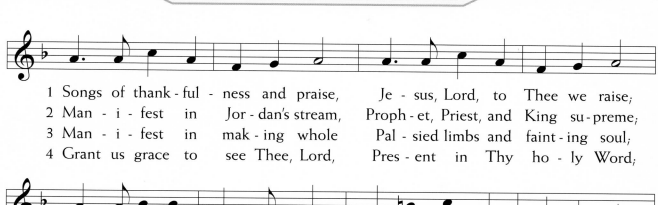

1 Songs of thank - ful - ness and praise,   Je - sus, Lord, to Thee we raise;
2 Man - i - fest   in   Jor - dan's stream,   Proph - et, Priest, and King su - preme;
3 Man - i - fest   in   mak - ing whole   Pal - sied limbs and faint - ing soul;
4 Grant us grace to   see Thee, Lord,   Pres - ent in Thy ho - ly Word;

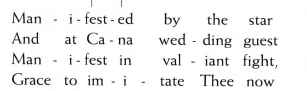

Man - i - fest - ed   by   the   star   To   the   sa - ges   from a - far,
And   at Ca - na   wed - ding guest   In   Thy God-head   man - i - fest;
Man - i - fest in   val - iant fight,   Quell - ing   all   the   dev - il's might;
Grace to im - i - tate Thee now   And   be   pure, as   pure art Thou;

Branch of roy - al   Da - vid's stem   In   Thy birth at   Beth - le - hem:
Man - i - fest in   pow'r di - vine,   Chang - ing wa - ter   in - to wine;
Man - i - fest in   gra - cious will,   Ev - er bring-ing   good from ill;
That   we might be - come like Thee   At   Thy great e - pi - pha - ny

An - thems be   to   Thee ad-dressed,   God in flesh made man - i - fest.
An - thems be   to   Thee ad-dressed,   God in flesh made man - i - fest.
An - thems be   to   Thee ad-dressed,   God in flesh made man - i - fest.
And   may praise Thee,   ev - er blest,   God in flesh made man - i - fest.

Text: Christopher Wordsworth, 1807–85
Tune: ST. GEORGE'S, WINDSOR, George J. Elvey, 1816–93

Peppermint Star Brittle

⭐ 2 lbs. white chocolate
⭐ 30 peppermint star candies

Line a baking sheet with heavy-duty foil.

Unwrap candies and place in heavy-duty plastic bag or between two pieces of waxed paper. Using a mallet or rolling pin, break the candy into chunks. Set aside.

Place the chocolate in the top of a double boiler, and melt over low to medium heat, stirring constantly, until chocolate is melted. Or place chocolate in large microwave-safe bowl. Heat in microwave oven on medium setting for five to six minutes, stirring frequently, until chocolate is melted.

Stir crushed candy into melted white chocolate. Spread evenly in foil-lined pan and chill in refrigerator until set, about one hour.

Break brittle into pieces by slamming pan on counter.

Graham Cracker Treasure Boxes

⭐ Graham crackers
⭐ Cake icing in various colors
⭐ Decorations, such as red hots, silver balls, sprinkles, gum drops, and small coated chocolate candies

Each box uses six graham cracker squares. Build the box by "gluing" the graham crackers together at right angles to make a box. Before attaching the lid, place a sweet surprise inside the box. Use more icing to attach the lid. Then decorate the top of the treasure box with more icing and decorations.

Use these boxes as place cards at a special Epiphany dinner. Or make them as part of a family devotional activity.

Long ago and far away
    some thinkers—very wise—
Each evening watched the sun go down;
    they watched the starry skies.

They knew the moon; they knew each star;
    they studied planets, too.
The Wise Men drew their charts and maps;
    their wisdom grew and grew.

One night as darkness dimmed the light
    and stars began to shine,
Appeared a brand new star to them—
    a star so big and fine.

The Wise Men knew a special joy;
    they shouted out, "Prepare!
This star can only mean one thing:
    a King is born! But where?"

They left their homes to find that King;
    they carried gifts of love.
The star shone brightly on their way,
    a brilliant guide above.

'Twas Jesus whom they rightly sought;
    'twas Herod whom they found—
The king of all Jerusalem,
    the meanest man around.

The Wise Men asked King Herod, "Where,
    oh, where's this newborn king?
We want to worship Him with love,
    to Him our praises sing."

But wicked Herod couldn't say
    where Jesus had been born.
He did not know, he could not tell
    what happened Christmas morn.

So Herod told his scholars, "You
    must look for all you're worth
In ev'ry book and scroll to learn
    this place of kingly birth."

They answered, "Yes! In Bethlehem,
    King David's family town—
That must be where this Babe lives now."
    (King Herod hid his frown.)

That awful king paced back and forth;
    he was a jealous man!
"Another king will take my crown,"
    he thought. Then made a plan:

"Please go and find this King," he said,
    "then hurry back and say
Exactly where He lives so I
    can worship Him some day."

King Herod's very wicked heart
    had blurted out this lie.
He'd never worship Jesus Christ;
    he wanted Him to die!

The Wise Men left Jerusalem
    to go to Bethlehem,
And in the darkened sky they saw
    the star, still guiding them.

So they rejoiced with happy hearts;
    with hope they traveled fast
Until they saw the star stand still—
    they'd found the Child at last!

In front of Jesus, bowing down,
    they praised their Savior-Lord.
With gifts of gold and frankincense
    and myrrh He was adored.

Then in a dream that night they heard
    the voice of God say, "Go,
Returning home another way,
    but not to Herod! No!"

The Wise Men did what God had said,
    though Herod's anger grew;
For Jesus, Savior, Son of God,
    had godly work to do.

FROM *THE VISIT OF THE WISE MEN*

May the story of Christmas be told among us as long as we gather as God's people. May we hear it with the joy of children and tell it with the hope of those whose salvation is sure. May Christmas light and life and love be yours this day and always. In the name of the Father and the Son and the Holy Spirit. Amen.

FROM *Because of Christmas*

ACKNOWLEDGEMENTS, CREDITS

PAGE 10

"As man longs" from *Jesus, Joy of Man's Desiring*, F. H. Rogner, copyright © 1964 Concordia Publishing House, St. Louis, Missouri.

PAGE 11

"At Christmas time" from *He Came*, copyright © 1963 Concordia Publishing House, St. Louis, Missouri.

"Saint Nicholas" from *Emmanuel, God with Us! Family Devotions for Advent*, Henry Gerike, copyright © 2003 Concordia Publishing House, St. Louis, Missouri.

PAGE 14

"Long ago one holy night" from *Gifts for Jesus*, Mary L. Brummer, copyright © 1966 Concordia Publishing House, St. Louis, Missouri.

PAGE 17

"From heaven came" from "From Heaven Came the Angels Bright" (*Lutheran Worship* 52:1), Martin Luther, copyright © 1982 Concordia Publishing House, St. Louis, Missouri.

PAGE 22

"Lying in a manger see" from *The REAL Meaning of Christmas*, Ruth C. Werning, copyright © 1963 Concordia Publishing House, St. Louis, Missouri.

"The Christ who came at Christmas" from *He Came*, copyright © 1963 Concordia Publishing House, St. Louis, Missouri.

PAGE 24

"Do you ever get the feeling" from *The Baby Born in a Stable*, Janice Kramer, copyright © 1965 Concordia Publishing House, St. Louis, Missouri.

PAGE 26

"Of the shepherds we are told" from *Let Us Now Go Even unto Bethlehem*, copyright © 1966 Concordia Publishing House, St. Louis, Missouri.

PAGE 30

"Wake Up, Brother, Listen" from *Sing Peace, Sing Gift of Peace* 382, Jaroslav J. Vajda, copyright © 2003 Concordia Publishing House, St. Louis, Missouri.

"The story of our Savior's birth" adapted from *On a Silent Night*, Joy Morgan Davis, copyright © 2000 Concordia Publishing House, St. Louis, Missouri.

PAGE 33

"Little Baby in the Cradle" from *The REAL Meaning of Christmas*, Ruth C. Werning, copyright © 1963 Concordia Publishing House, St. Louis, Missouri.

"In the thirteenth century" adapted from *Signs and Symbols of Christmas*, Fritz A. Callies, copyright © 1966 Concordia Publishing House, St. Louis, Missouri.

"Baby Jesus" from *Signs and Symbols of Christmas*, Fritz A. Callies, copyright © 1966 Concordia Publishing House, St. Louis, Missouri.

PAGE 34

"We've a Story to Tell" from *We've a Story to Tell*, Mary L. Brummer, copyright © 1982 Concordia Publishing House, St. Louis, Missouri.

PAGE 36

"Angels were the first to sing" adapted from *Children Sing of Christmas*, Dean Nadasdy, copyright © 1982 Concordia Publishing House, St. Louis, Missouri.

PAGE 38

"Much is said about 'peace' these days" adapted from *On Earth Peace*, H. W. Gockel and E. J. Saleska, copyright © 1964 Concordia Publishing House, St. Louis, Missouri.

PAGE 40

"Silent night, holy night" adapted from *Unto Us a Savior*, copyright © 1966 Concordia Publishing House, St. Louis, Missouri.

PAGE 42

"On a Silent Night" from *On a Silent Night*, Joy Morgan Davis, copyright © 2000 Concordia Publishing House, St. Louis, Missouri.

PAGE 44

"Bethlehem, which means 'house of bread'" adapted from *Emmanuel, God with Us! Family Devotions for Advent*, Henry Gerike, copyright © 2003 Concordia Publishing House, St. Louis, Missouri.

PAGE 46

"Once in royal David's city" from "Once in Royal David's City" (*Lutheran Service Book* 376:1), Cecil F. Alexander, copyright © 2006 Concordia Publishing House, St. Louis, Missouri.

PAGE 47

"O holy Child of Bethlehem" from "O Little Town of Bethlehem" (*Lutheran Service Book* 361:4), Phillips Brooks, copyright © 2006 Concordia Publishing House, St. Louis, Missouri.

PAGE 48

"Christmas isn't only A decorated tree" from *Come, Lord Jesus*, Ruth S. Hummel, copyright © 1964 Concordia Publishing House, St. Louis, Missouri.

"Sweetest Song of This Bright Season" from *Sing Peace, Sing Gift of Peace* 456, Hector Hoppe, copyright © 2003 Concordia Publishing House, St. Louis, Missouri.

"Come, children all, with one accord" from *On Earth Peace*, H. W. Gockel and E. J. Saleska, copyright © 1964 Concordia Publishing House, St. Louis, Missouri.

PAGE 50

"The air is filled with the music of Christmas" adapted from *Christmas Joy*, William A. Kramer, copyright © 1965 Concordia Publishing House, St. Louis, Missouri.

ILLUSTRATIONS

In a manger Jesus lies;
Angels praise Him in the skies.
Shepherds kneel before Him low.
To His stable let us go.
Light of heaven and Morning Star,
Dear Lord Jesus, Thine we are.
Lead us as Thy very own
To the Father's shining throne.

FROM CHRISTMAS JOY